Life in the Old West

HOMES OF THE WEST

Bobbie Kalman

 Crabtree Publishing Company

www.crabtreebooks.com

LIFE IN THE OLD WEST

Created by Bobbie Kalman

To Mark Vcislo
–traveler

Author and Editor-in-Chief
Bobbie Kalman

Managing editor
Lynda Hale

Senior editor
April Fast

Research and editing team
Ellen Groskorth
Marsha Baddeley
Jane Lewis
Kate Calder
Heather Levigne

Computer design
Lynda Hale
Robert MacGregor (cover concept)
Campbell Creative Services

Photo research
Marsha Baddeley

Production coordinator
Hannelore Sotzek

Special thanks to
Mary Helmich, California State Parks; Katrina Hoover and Sutter's Fort State Historic Park; William B. Ide Adobe State Historic Park; Pioneer Arizona Living History Museum; Marshall Gold Discovery State Historic Park; Tanque Verde Ranch; The CRB Foundation Heritage Project; Jim Bowman, Glenbow Archives; Montana Historical Society; George Robbins

Photographs and reproductions
Glenbow Archives, Calgary: title page, page 7 (bottom); George H. H. Huey: page 16; Jourdan-Bachman Pioneer Farm: pages 15 (top left), 23 (bottom); Bobbie Kalman, taken at Pioneer Arizona: pages 13, 15 (top right, bottom both), 19, 20 (both), 29 (middle, bottom both); *The Waterhole* ©1993 Tom Lovell, The Greenwich Workshop®, Inc. (detail): pages 4-5; *The Handwarmer* ©1993 Tom Lovell, The Greenwich Workshop®, Inc. (detail): pages 10-11; Montana Historical Society, Helena/ Evelyn J. Cameron: pages 12, 18, 21; Montana Historical Society, Helena/ L.A. Huffman: page 23 (top); National Cowboy Hall of Fame, Oklahoma City: page 10 (bottom); Nebraska State Historical Society: page 8; Nebraska State Historical Society/Solomon D. Butcher Collection: pages 9, 22 (bottom); James P. Rowan: pages 7 (top), 26; Tony & Alba Sanches-Zinnanti: pages 14, 28 (both), 29 (top)

Illustrations and colorizations
Barbara Bedell: pages 6, 7, 8, 14, 15, 19, 24-25, 27
Bonna Rouse: cover, pages 12, 13, 16-17, 30-31

Crabtree Publishing Company

PMB 16A
350 Fifth Ave.,
Suite 3308
N.Y., N.Y. 10118

612 Welland Ave.,
St. Catharines,
Ontario, Canada
L2M 5V6

73 Lime Walk
Headington
Oxford OX3 7AD
United Kingdom

Cataloging in Publication Data
Kalman, Bobbie
   Homes of the west

(Life in the Old West)
Includes index.
ISBN 0-7787-0074-7 (library bound) ISBN 0-7787-0106-9 (pbk.)
This book discusses types of homes in western North America in the 19th century, their construction, and the settlers who lived in them.
1. West (North America)—Social life and customs—Juvenile literature. 2. Dwellings—West (North America)—History—19th century—Juvenile literature. 3. Pioneers—West (North America)—Social life and customs—19th century—Juvenile literature. 4. Frontier and pioneer life—West (North America)—Juvenile literature. [1. Dwellings—West (North America)—History—19th century. 2. Frontier and pioneer life—West (North America) 3. West (North America)—Social life and customs.]
I. Title. II. Series: Kalman, Bobbie. Life in the Old West.
F596.K353 1999   j978   LC 98-37626
                          CIP

TABLE OF CONTENTS

OLD LAND, NEW HOMES

When Europeans first came to North America, they settled along the east coast. Towns and cities developed and grew as the population increased. During the 1800s, settlers began moving west to buy land and build new homes.

The challenge of building

Settlers built homes in valleys, mountain areas, forests, deserts, and on the plains. When they arrived in the west, they faced many challenges in building a home. They brought few tools with them, and there were no towns where they could buy supplies.

Logs, soil, or clay?

The settlers had to learn how to build homes by using materials they found in nature. In areas with many trees, settlers built log homes. In the prairies, where wood was scarce, they built houses using grass-covered soil. In desert areas, settlers used clay to make bricks for their home.

The First Peoples

The settlers were not the first people to live in the west. Native Americans had been living there for thousands of years! Native Americans refers to the aboriginal people of North America, once called Indians. They are also referred to as First Peoples. Native Nations and First Nations refers to the groups to which they belong, such as Cherokee or Cree.

Who owned the land?

Native Americans and the European settlers had different ways of life. Native Americans lived in harmony with nature.

They respected the land and the animals that shared it with them. Until the Europeans came, Native Americans did not believe people could own land any more than they could own the sky above it. When the settlers came, they built houses on the homelands of the Native Americans. They claimed this land as their property. Thousands of settlers continued to move west to build homes on this land.

The first meetings between the settlers and Native Americans were peaceful. They were curious about each other. This Native American man had never seen this type of well and wondered how the settlers got water out of a wooden box.

NATIVE DWELLINGS

The Native Americans who lived in the west built many types of **dwellings**, or homes. They made homes of stones, clay, wood, or buffalo hide.

Suited to a way of life

Each style of home suited the landscape, climate, and way of life of the people who built it. Some Native Nations built permanent homes, and others lived in moveable tentlike dwellings called **tipis**.

Different homes

Some Native Nations were **nomadic**—they did not live in one location permanently. Other Nations were farmers who built permanent homes on the land.

Tipis

Buffalo hunters of the Great Plains lived in tipis such as the one shown here. A tipi was made of buffalo hides and long wooden poles. Bone pins held the hide together. An opening was left for the door. Two flaps on the top of the tipi allowed air in and smoke out. Native Americans often painted pictures on their tipis. The pictures showed images from dreams.

Movable homes

The tipi was an ideal home for the nomadic Nations that lived on the plains. They moved around following herds of buffalo, which they hunted for their meat, bones, and skin. Tipis could be taken apart easily and carried to a new location.

Blackfoot, Crow, and Sioux are a few of the Nations that lived in tipis.

Earth lodges

Other Native Nations that lived on the plains, such as the Pawnee, built lodges of earth. Earth kept the lodge cool in summer and warm in winter. **Earth lodges** were permanent homes built by farmers.

The earth lodge to the right has just been built. Over time, grass will grow over the lodge, making it look like a small hill. The earth lodge below was built a long time ago.

Longhouses

Some of the Native Americans on the northwest coast lived in **longhouses**. Longhouses were large, rectangular homes made of cedar boards. Several families lived in each longhouse. Haida, Kwakiutl, Salish, Tsimshian, and Tlingit were some of the Nations that built longhouses.

*(below) The Haida Nation decorated their dwellings with intricately carved poles called **totem poles**.*

BUILDING A "SODDY"

(top) This large family lives in one soddy.
(bottom) Small sod shelters were built for animals.

Some of the first homes built by settlers on the plains or prairies were made of **sod**. Sod is a section of grass and soil. Settlers had to use sod "bricks" because there were not enough trees on the plains to build houses out of wood.

Sod homes were not fancy, but they were easy to build. The thick walls of earth kept out the winter cold. A sod home was also less likely to burn down than a house made of wood. Sod homes were nicknamed "soddies."

A soddy for Peter and John

Peter and John were covered in dirt. They were standing in the creek in their bare feet, throwing handfuls of mud at each other. When their mother came to investigate, she hardly recognized her sons. "O.K., boys," she said, "let's get back to work!"

Peter and John were helping their parents build a sod house. Their job was to dig up mud from the creek. The mud would be used to hold the bricks together. While the boys were digging, their father cut sod bricks out of the ground with his shovel. The square bricks were covered with grass.

When the sod bricks were ready, everyone helped pile them up, layer by layer, on the spot chosen for the house. Peter and John were careful to keep the walls straight and even. To hold the bricks together, they spread mud between them.

Father made wooden frames for the doors and windows and left spaces for them. After the frames were put in place, the rest of the bricks were used to finish the walls. Peter and John could not help place the last bricks on the walls because they were too small to carry the heavy sod bricks up the ladder.

It was now time to build the roof. Mother and Father placed a wooden frame on top of the sod walls and made up a game for the children. Peter and John had to run in from the field carrying a bundle of hay. They raced to see who would be the first to get their bundle to their mother! When their mother received a bundle, she climbed up the ladder and handed the hay to their father, who placed it over the wooden frame. Then the race started all over again. After the frame was completely covered with hay, Mother and Father finished the roof by laying sod bricks over it.

The sod home was finally ready! The boys and their sisters would no longer have to sleep in the wagon. They would sleep indoors on straw beds. Peter and John were happy to have a new home and proud that they had helped Mother and Father build it.

Dugout Homes

Not all settlers built a home as soon as they arrived. Some lived in temporary shelters until they finished clearing the land and planting crops. They had plenty of time to build a house after the other work was done. **Dugouts** often served as a temporary shelter. They were "dug out" of the ground or hillside. A dugout resembled the earth lodge of the Pawnee, even though it was made differently. Some newcomers were fortunate enough to find a dugout on their land. Sometimes miners or traders who had moved on had abandoned theirs.

Digging a dugout

To build a dugout, settlers scooped earth out of the side of a hill, making a cave. The cave formed the back, sides, and roof of the home. An entrance or front wall was then built using sod, stones, or wood—whatever material was available. An open space was left for a door, which was made of a buffalo hide, wool blanket, or wooden poles that were lashed together. Some dugouts, such as the one shown in the painting, had a proper door and windows. This dugout home even had a stove for cooking and heating.

The finishing touches

The dirt floor of the dugout was packed down hard to give it a smooth finish. Windows were small and covered with paper, animal skins, or wood. Some settlers **whitewashed**, or painted the walls with ashes, clay, or plaster. Other settlers covered the walls with newspaper, old clothes, or paper.

It was very cold outside, and these two travelers were delighted to find a hot spot to warm their hands. The settlers inside the dugout must have wondered who or what was walking across their roof!

PUTTING UP A LOG HOME

In areas where there were many trees, the settlers built log homes. Log homes were much more stable and lasted longer than sod homes. They were also cleaner! It took a long time and a lot of energy to build a log house, but it was worth the effort.

Turning a forest into a home

It took the pioneers several weeks to cut down enough trees to build a log house. After the trees were felled, the logs were stripped of their bark and cut to the same length. They were laid one on top of the other to form a rectangular or square shape. With help from neighbors and friends, settlers lifted the logs into place.

*Notches were made at the ends of the logs so that they would fit tightly together. The notch shown in the drawing is called a **saddle notch**. Can you guess why?*

This settler is adding a room to his house. His brother and wife have just arrived in the west and need a place to live. It will not be as lonely with family so close by. The nearest neighbors are miles away!

Dirt or wooden floors

The floor of the log house was made of dirt or **puncheons**. Puncheons were large logs that had been split in half. The flat side was sanded down to make it smooth. The puncheons were laid over the dirt with their flat side facing up.

Small windows

Doors and windows were cut out of the log walls with a saw. Windows were usually small. In the winter, it was important to keep heat inside the house and small windows let out less heat than larger ones. Settlers who did not have glass windowpanes used animal skins, greased paper, or wooden shutters to cover the windows.

Doors and verandahs

The door was made of wood and hung from wooden hinges or leather straps along one side. In winter, buffalo hides were draped over the door to keep out the cold. In areas where the summers were hot, the settlers built a **verandah**, or roofed porch, to provide shade.

The roof and chimney

The roof of a log house was covered with hand-cut boards or shingles called **shakes**. The first fireplace was often made of logs. The inside of the chimney was coated with mud or clay to keep it from catching fire. Even with a clay lining, however, a log fireplace was a fire hazard. As soon as they had the materials and time, settlers removed their old fireplace and built a new one out of stone.

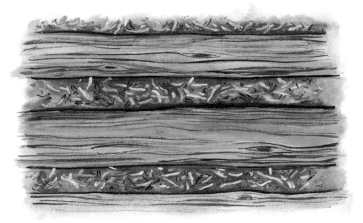

The spaces between the logs needed to be filled with wood chips, moss, mud, or clay to keep out wind and rain.

INSIDE A LOG CABIN

The interior of a log home was plain and simple. The first settlers brought only a few pieces of furniture with them on their long journey west. They had to make the furniture they needed by hand after they arrived at their new home. Settlers used natural materials to decorate and heat their home.

The fireplace

The main source of heat and light in early homes was the fireplace. If the settlers did not have a stove, the fireplace was also used for cooking.

Keeping the home fires burning

On the plains and in desert areas, very little wood was available. Settlers burned grass, hay, scrub bushes, and dried animal dung for cooking food and heating the home. Stoves called **hay burners** were used to burn hay.

Simple furnishings

Shelves for storage and pegs for hanging clothes were added after the home was built. Soon after moving in, the settlers made tables, stools, benches, and chests for storing blankets and clothes. Rope beds and straw mattresses provided a comfortable place to sleep.

(left) Many settlers pasted newspapers on the inside walls of their log cabin to keep out the cold air and rain.

(below) The first beds were made of wood and rope with a mattress laid on top.

(above) If a carpenter lived nearby, the settlers were able to buy simple tables and cabinets to furnish their home.

(right) On cool evenings, families often gathered around the fireplace to tell stories.

Adobe Homes

When settlers first arrived in the Southwest, they found few materials with which to build homes. The land was dry, and the climate was hot. There were no forests, and there was no grass. The settlers could not build log or sod homes. Instead, they used **adobe** to construct their dwellings. Adobe is a Spanish word that means sun-dried clay. Adobe homes stayed cool during the day and retained the warmth of the sun at night.

Building an adobe house

The settlers made adobe bricks from clay and water. They added sand, plant roots, and straw to make the bricks stronger and poured the mixture into rectangular wooden molds. The bricks were left to harden and dry in the sun. The settlers stacked the bricks to form thick walls and used clay to fill the spaces between them. Adobe was then plastered over the walls to make them look smooth. Floors were also made of adobe. Settlers sometimes mixed animal blood into the clay to make it hard and keep it from turning into mud when it rained.

Shady shelter

Summers in the desert could get very hot and dry. To find shelter from the heat, the settlers built a verandah. Some people had a courtyard at the side or back of the house that was enclosed by a wall, which also provided shade.

Still a good thing

Adobe is still used as a building material in the Southwest. This material is inexpensive and strong. Homes made of adobe are now called Santa Fe-style homes, named after the capital city of New Mexico.

Pueblos

Long before the settlers arrived, Native Nations such as the Zuni, Hopi, and Taos built adobe and stone homes called *pueblos*. *Pueblos*, such as the one above, had several levels and rooms. There were no doors on the first level. Ladders were used to get into the upper rooms and could easily be pulled up to keep out intruders. *Pueblo* means village, people, or nation. The people who lived in *pueblos* were also called *Pueblos*. They planted crops and made pottery and rugs.

Frame Houses

A **frame house** was built around a structure or frame. The settlers started by making the frame from wood and nailing **planks**, or boards, side by side against it. The first frame homes were made using thick, uneven planks. The early settlers cut the planks with a handsaw. It took a long time and a lot of work to cut enough planks to build a house.

Hurray for sawmills!

Sawmills made it much easier for settlers to build frame homes. A sawmill cut logs into boards using machine-powered saws. The wood cut at the sawmill was very straight, so the frames were even, and the planks could be placed tightly together. The evenly placed planks kept out wind and rain.

This settler and her husband are proud of their tiny plank home on the prairie. The husband has just returned from a successful hunting trip, and the wife will cook rabbit stew for dinner.

New and improved

Mill-cut planks were thin and light and allowed settlers to improve their homes in several ways. Using planks, the settlers could build a two-story home. The settlers were also able to divide their home into several rooms, including a kitchen, dining room, and bedrooms.

Wilderness, village, or town?

Some frame homes were plain, and others were fancy. Study these three photographs and write a description about each of the communities in which these homes might have been located.

Life in the west was more comfortable in a frame home. Turn the page, and find out why!

Frame homes made the lives of the settlers more comfortable and enjoyable. They were easier to keep clean and decorate because the floors and walls were smooth. Smooth walls were also easier to paint. Many people put wallpaper on the walls to make their rooms look more attractive.

The furniture in frame homes was often made by a cabinet maker or came from a furniture factory.

The kitchen

The kitchen was the warmest room in the house. Instead of a fireplace, most frame homes had a stove. The stove did a better job of heating the home. Cooking on a stove was also easier and safer than cooking over a fire.

The kitchen was a busy place! Cooking, eating, doing laundry, candle making, reading, talking, and singing all took place in this room. In the winter, people bathed in the kitchen because it was warm there. The kitchen was the most important room in the house. It was the heart of the home.

Bedrooms of their own

Frame homes had several bedrooms. The room in which the parents slept was usually next to the kitchen. It was a warm room, so babies and young children sometimes slept in this room as well. The kitchen stove heated the whole house, but the upstairs bedrooms were often chilly in winter.

The parlor

Many homes had a **parlor**. The parlor was the best room in the house. Women did their sewing in the parlor, and the family read the Bible there on Sundays. It was the room in which families entertained important guests.

*This parlor has a loveseat. It was called a **courting chair**. When **courting**, or dating, a couple could sit and talk in this chair without being too close!*

This kitchen made of planks has been added onto the settler's first home, which was made from logs. The smooth floors could be kept clean easily. This addition has a stove instead of a fireplace, making it less work to cook a meal.

EARLY RANCHES

A ranch was home to many people who lived in the west. It was like a big farm. Instead of growing crops, ranchers raised sheep, cows, or horses. Most ranches in the west, however, raised cattle for their meat. Many ranches started out small—with one or two buildings. As time passed, the ranches grew bigger.

The ranch house

Some early ranch houses were made of logs, sod, or clay bricks. If there was a sawmill in the area, ranchers used planks to construct their home. As their business expanded, ranchers and their families built a larger home. The rancher's home was called the **main house**.

This early cattle ranch had only two main buildings—a house and barn. The small house behind the barn might have been a tool shed or milk house.

The bunkhouse

When a ranch increased in size, the rancher hired cowboys to help herd the cattle and make repairs. The cowboys slept in a separate house called a **bunkhouse**. Large ranches had several bunkhouses.

A simple home

Bunkhouses usually had one big room with few furnishings. Some had bunk beds, whereas others had no beds at all—the cowboys slept on the floor. Pegs on the walls held their clothes and other belongings.

The mess hall

Cowboys worked hard and had a big appetite! They ate their meals in the cook house or **mess hall**. Long wooden tables and benches were set up to seat all the men. The meals were cooked by the rancher's wife or a hired cook.

*The top picture shows the inside of a bunkhouse. The cowboy has hung his belongings on pegs. The bunkhouse and mess hall were often connected by a **dogtrot**. A dogtrot is a hallway with a roof over it, such as the one shown in the bottom picture.*

LATER RANCHES

Many ranches grew to be huge. Some ranchers owned thousands of acres of land on which their cattle grazed. They built new houses for the cowboys and barns for the horses and other animals. The later buildings were not made from sod or logs. They were built with planks. The buildings were located close together and formed a small community.

A fancy main house

Wealthy ranchers had a large, well-furnished, comfortable main house. Main houses often had a long verandah. The house had a dining room, large kitchen, and several bedrooms. A small room was used as an office by the rancher. Many ranch houses also had a parlor. The parlor was reserved for entertaining guests.

Hay, quit stalling. I need straw!

Horses were kept in stables. Each horse had its own stall with fresh straw for bedding. The stalls also had hay for the horses to eat. It was important for horses to have a warm, dry place to sleep. They needed to stay healthy because they did much of the heavy work on a ranch.

Hay and straw were kept dry in a large, open shed. Each day a cowboy cleaned out the stalls and brought the horses fresh hay and straw.

The blacksmith shed

Ranchers had many horses, and horses needed horseshoes to protect their hoofs. The blacksmith made horseshoes in a shed. He **shod** the horses, or put the horseshoes on their hoofs. The blacksmith also made and repaired tools, cooking utensils, barrel hoops, locks, and nails. When someone had a bad tooth, the blacksmith used his tools to pull it out!

Corrals for training horses

The **corral** was a fenced area used for **breaking**, or taming, wild horses. It was close to the stables. Most corrals were round so the horses would not back into the corners and make it hard for the cowboys to pull them out and ride them.

Windmills for pumping water

Ranches needed a lot of water for cooking, bathing, and washing. The people and animals also needed water for drinking. Few ranches were built on the shores of lakes or rivers. Ranchers had to find water underground and then build a well. When the well was ready, the best way to pump water up from the ground was to use a windmill for power. This ranch has two windmills.

Food for the family and cowboys

Ranches were far from towns and farms, so they needed to be **self-sufficient**. They had to provide the rancher's family and the cowboys with everything they needed, including tools, food, and supplies such as soap and candles. The ranchers had a field and orchard for growing fruit and vegetables.

The main house at this ranch has two stories, but many ranch houses were long with only one floor of living space. Today, when people talk about a ranch-style home, they refer to a rectangular one-story home.

As more people arrived in the west, towns began to grow and develop. Mills, factories, stores, and other businesses opened. Many business owners became wealthy and built large, fancy houses to show off their success. They paid great attention to detail in building their homes. Both the outside and the inside of the home had to look good.

Victorian homes

The fancy houses built in the second half of the 19th century were called Victorian homes. Some were made of bricks and others of planks. The yellow home on page 19 is a small Victorian house made of planks. The Victorian home shown on page 26 is a large two-story home made of bricks. It has **gables**, a **turret**, and a **wraparound** porch. Living in a Victorian home made westerners feel more "civilized" and less homesick for the east.

Many Victorian homes had libraries containing expensive collections of leather-bound books.

This chest could be closed to hide the basin and pitcher that were used for washing.

To keep the furniture and curtains smelling fresh, men were allowed to smoke only in the smoking room.

*Victorian homes were lit by hand-painted oil lamps and fancy **chandeliers**.*

*Many Victorian home owners kept plants and caged birds in a **conservatory**, or greenhouse.*

Victorian furniture was made of intricately carved wood and covered with fine fabrics.

The early settlers of the west had to make everything they needed from scratch because there were no shops where they could buy supplies such as soap and candles.

Soap- and candle-making

The first step in making soap and candles was to boil animal fat and water together in a kettle. This melted fat was called **tallow**. To make soap, settlers added **lye** to the tallow. Lye is a liquid made by dripping water through ashes. The lye and tallow mixture was poured into a pan and left to harden overnight.

Tallow was also used to make candles. Settlers dipped candlewicks made of string into the melted fat. When the wick was pulled out, a layer of tallow remained on the wick. After it dried, the string was dipped again until the candle was the right thickness.

(top) These children are making candles. Each time they dip a wick into the tallow, it gets a little thicker. They will dip their wicks many times before their candles are done.

(bottom) These bars of soap were made from the animal fat shown beside the box. Sometimes honey, pine, or ginger was added to candles and soap to make them smell good.

Outdoor ovens

In many places, it was too hot to cook indoors during the summer, so families had outdoor ovens. The oven was used for baking bread, buns, muffins, and cakes.

Outhouses

Throughout most of the 1800s, there was no plumbing or running water inside houses. Toilets were built outdoors, a short distance away from the house. Outdoor toilets were called **outhouses**. An outhouse was a narrow shack with a door and a small window. A hole was dug in the ground beneath it, and inside, there was a platform or seat above the hole.

Many homes had boot scrapers outside their front door to clean off the mud and animal waste from shoes and boots.

Hitching posts were like bicycle racks. They were everywhere! Instead of leaving bikes, people tied horses to these handy parking spots.

DANGERS OF WESTERN LIFE

Living in the west was often more difficult than people ever imagined! Settlers had to face new challenges and cope with unexpected dangers. Diseases such as **typhoid**, **malaria**, and **cholera** were a great problem because there were few doctors to help people who got sick or hurt. Accidents, weather conditions, and wild or poisonous creatures also added to the daily drama of life in the old west.

Guess who's coming to dinner?

Living in a sod house or dugout could be risky! When it rained, the roof leaked and often caved in on top of the people living inside. Since a dugout was built into the side of a hill, sometimes a cow or horse walking over it came crashing through the roof. Have you ever had a cow drop in for dinner? Surprise!

Dangerous guests

Settlers in the Southwest learned to live with unfamiliar and dangerous creatures. They checked to make sure there were no rattlesnakes coiled up under the beds or between their sheets. Rattlesnake bites could be deadly! Scorpions and huge spiders called tarantulas often hid in people's shoes or boots. A tarantula bite was not as dangerous as a bite from a scorpion. Scorpion bites could kill small children!

Skunks and coyotes also caused problems for the settlers. Skunks stole food and sprayed animals with a smelly liquid. Coyotes ate farm animals. In some areas, settlers had to watch out for bears!

Fire and wind

Many chimneys were made of logs or other material that burned easily. Stone or brick fireplaces could also cause a home to fill up with smoke or catch on fire if they did not work properly. Chimney fires occurred when soot or a bird's nest blocked the chimney.

Severe heat and lack of rain caused fires to rage across the land and destroy homes. Dust storms, tornadoes, and blizzards were other natural threats that settlers faced.

The settler who owns these boots had better look inside them before he gets dressed! A scorpion is hiding there!

GLOSSARY

chandelier A fancy light fixture that hangs from the ceiling

cholera A disease that causes diarrhea, vomiting, cramps, and dehydration

dwelling A place where a person lives; a home

frame house A house built around a supporting structure

gable A triangular feature of a building, used as decoration over a door or window

Great Plains A large area of flat, grass-covered land located in central North America

hinge A joint that holds a door to a door frame and allows it to swing open and shut

lye A strong liquid made from water and wood ashes that is used to make soap

malaria A disease that causes fever and chills

mill A building with machines that turn raw materials into a finished product

nomadic Describing people who move from place to place

plank A piece of sawed wood

prairie An area of flat, grass-covered land

sawmill A factory where logs are cut by machines

self-sufficient Able to take care of oneself

Southwest An area of the southwestern United States that covers New Mexico, Arizona, California, Texas, and Nevada

tallow Melted animal fat used to make soap and candles

turret A small tower on a house or building

typhoid A disease that is transmitted by consuming bad water or food and causes fever, headache, coughing, and skin rash

utensil An object or tool used in the kitchen

Victorian Describing houses, furnishings, or objects that are highly ornamented

whitewash To cover walls with a white, paintlike liquid

wraparound Describing something that surrounds another thing

INDEX

3 4 5 6 7 8 9 0   Printed in the U.S.A.   7 6 5 4 3 2 1